Understanding the
Crowning Ceremony
of the Coptic Orthodox Church

DEACON VICTOR BESHIR

The Parthenos Press

Contents

"Rejoice and be glad, beloved, and blessed bridegroom and your blessed bride, because you have attained great grace, and have been adorned with a heavenly spiritual garment, through this glorious mystery.

"The grace of the Holy Spirit, the issuer of all fine gifts, has descended upon you, unifying you into one person.

"Thus, it is befitting to congratulate you with the hymns of joy and voices of jubilation.

"Rejoice because of this gift that God has bestowed upon you and receive with gratitude and glorification this honor granted to you from above, since you have been crowned with the crown of honor and pride, the crown of joy and delight."

(From the exposition prayers recited during the removal of the crowns, which used to take place a few days after the marriage ceremony)

Foreword

to the First Edition

In his Epistle to the Ephesians, St. Paul says about the Mystery of Matrimony: "This is a great mystery, but I speak concerning Christ and the church" (Eph 5:32). The greatness of this mystery springs from the fact that God Himself instituted it when He blessed Adam and Eve when He created them, and when Christ launched His ministry with the miracle of turning the water into wine at the wedding of Cana of Galilee.

There is a figurative meaning behind the turning of water into wine. Water symbolizes the power that strives to quench the love between the husband and the wife, as mentioned in the Song of Songs: "Many waters cannot quench love, nor can the floods drown it. If a man would give for love all the wealth of his house, it would be utterly despised" (Song 8:7).

On the other hand, wine signifies the strong love between them "For your love is better than wine" (Song 1:2). Christ was told, "They have no wine" (Jn 2:3). "Now there were set there six waterpots" (Jn 2:6). Love disappeared from this wedding, in the presence of many forces (six waterpots) of ego, selfishness, and the love of possessions that threatened this marriage. So, how is this problem solved?

Submitting to God in a spirit of humility and prayer fills the heart with a never-failing divine love capable of preserving the peace and unity of the family. "Because the love of God has been poured out in our hearts by the Holy Spirit who was given to us" (Rom 5:5). God has turned that destructive force that threatens the entity of the family (water) into a deep, fulfilling love (wine). That is why the Church repeatedly implores God, during the crowning ceremony, to bless the couple just as He blessed the wedding at Cana of Galilee, turning the water into wine.

This book is a contemplative spiritual study of the rites of the Mystery of Matrimony, written to help us understand the abundant blessings hidden within this holy mystery. We ask the Lord to use this book to bring fruit, and to bless the author, Deacon Victor Beshir, who worked tirelessly on this study, through the intercession of our Mother of God, St. Mary, and the prayers of all the saints and of Pope Shenouda the third.

Youssef,

Bishop of the Southern United States

October 13, 2002

Babah 21, 1719 A.M., Commemoration of the departure of St. Reweis

Foreword

to the Second Edition

The Mystery of marriage holds a profound place in the life of humanity from the very beginning of creation when the Lord created Adam and Eve and proclaimed, "A man shall leave his father and mother and be joined to his wife, and they shall become one flesh." (Gen 2:24). St. Paul comments on this verse later in the New Testament when speaking about the mystery of the husband and wife being united saying, "This is a great mystery, but I speak concerning Christ and the church." (Eph 5:32)

Therefore, the married couples are the nucleus of humanity and society, and likewise the nucleus of God's Church from the beginning. The "church in your house" (Rom 16:5; 1 Cor 16:19; Col 4:15; Philem. 2) that St. Paul often speaks about is the fabric from which comes the beautiful quilt of God's Church. In a world where the sanctity of this divine institution is increasingly challenged, there arises a spiritual need for resources such as the book in your hand, which remind believers of the deeper reality of the Mystery of marriage and its initiation in the Crowning Ceremony.

This book provides a comprehensive exploration of the Crowning Ceremony within the Coptic Orthodox Church. It delves into the rich symbolism of the rites, the theological significances, the prayers that invoke God's blessings upon the couple, and the responsibilities that the sacrament bestows upon them. The zealous author, Deacon Victor Beshir, has diligently compiled and explained these elements in a concise manner, a trait that I personally saw in him from long ago when I was exposed to his many pamphlets and small leaflets prepared for orthodox evangelism.

May the Lord bless Deacon Victor for his labor of love in compiling this work, and may the readers find in it a source of spiritual enrichment, leading them to a deeper understanding of the holy Mystery of marriage. May it inspire all who engage with it to live out the true essence of Christian matrimony, reflecting Christ's love and unity in their own lives, that Christ's prayer to the Father may be fulfilled: "that they may be made perfect in one, and that the world may know that You have sent Me, and have loved them as You have loved Me" (Jn 17:23).

Basil

By the grace of God,

Auxiliary Bishop in the Coptic Orthodox Diocese of the Southern United States

August 17, 2024

Mesra 11, 1740, The Departure of St. Moisis, Bishop of Ouseem.

Acknowledgement

I humbly express my profound gratitude to the Lord, whose divine guidance and grace have enabled me to complete this book. Without His support, this achievement would not have been possible. I attribute all that is commendable and valuable in this work to Him, while any shortcomings or deficiencies are solely my own.

I extend my heartfelt gratitude to His Eminence Metropolitan Youssef, Metropolitan of the Coptic Orthodox Diocese of the Southern United States, for his love, support, and invaluable contribution in reviewing the Arabic edition of this book and writing its Foreword. I am deeply indebted to His Grace Bishop Basil, Auxiliary Bishop in the Coptic Orthodox Diocese of the Southern United States, for his review of the English edition of this book and for writing the foreword to the second edition.

I would like to express my deepest gratitude to my wife, Lyla, and my daughter, Mary, for their unwavering support and encouragement throughout the journey of writing this book. Special thanks to Dr. Esmat Gabriel for reading the draft of the book and providing invaluable insights.

My gratitude goes to Mrs. Suhair Shenouda for her dedication and tireless efforts. I feel a deep sense of gratitude to Mrs. Suzan Hanna, whose countless hours of hard work have been instrumental in shaping this book into its final form.

Special thanks are due to Dr. Joseph Lotfi for his insightful remarks. I am grateful to Mr. Gerges Gad for his constructive suggestions.

I am also grateful to the monks of St. Mary and St. Moses Abbey in Texas for their diligent efforts in printing the book. May the Lord reward all those who assisted me until the book reached its readers.

Deacon Victor Beshir
April 7, 2024
Annunciation Feast

Prologue

What are these wonderful prayers?

You might have attended a Coptic Orthodox wedding ceremony before and wondered about the significance of these unique rituals and the profound prayers. The Coptic Orthodox Church has wonderful rituals that convey to us the image of heaven and allow us to taste its beauty while still here on earth. They transport us into spiritual realms that can't be described in words.

The prayers of the Coptic Orthodox wedding, called the Crowning Ceremony, lay before us abundant spiritual nourishment, and take us on a wonderful spiritual journey. I invite you to embark on this journey and taste its beauty every time you attend the Ceremony of the Holy Matrimony.

However, first, you need to know what happens during the Ceremony of the Holy Matrimony, the Crowning Ceremony, and understand the meaning of each prayer and rite. Only then will these prayers become like a ladder that our souls climb to reach spiritual heights and get closer to the Divine Throne.

This, my Dear Reader, is what I will try to present to you through this book in a simple yet appealing style. I wanted you to find it easy and interesting to sail through the pages and unravel the beauty of those prayers and their meaning.

This book presents the Crowning Ceremony as currently practiced in the Coptic Orthodox Church, according to the amendments approved by the Holy Synod, under the auspices of His Holiness Pope Shenouda III, on May 29, 1999. Throughout this book, expressions such as "in the past" or "the Church used to" are used to refer to earlier practices, whether from the recent or more distant past. I have written the prayers, hymns, and readings used in this ceremony in red font. Throughout the book, I use "Holy Matrimony" and "Crowning Ceremony" interchangeably to refer to the same ceremony: the former signifies the sacrament and the work of the Holy Spirit upon the bride and bridegroom, while the latter describes the liturgical ceremony as celebrated in the Church.

This book is an invitation to a deeper spiritual understanding of marriage, the ceremony's prayers, and the preparations that precede and follow it. Therefore, it may be used as a tool to prepare couples and their families before Marriage, and it may also serve as a meaningful gift from clergy, church meetings, or friends, either to couples getting married or to youth before marriage.

At the same time, this book is a call for a return to the inner depth of the rites of this ceremony as the Church once practiced them, and a plea to restore important elements in the Crowning Ceremony that have been lost or neglected over the years. It is a call to rediscover the Church's heritage, not merely for the sake of antiquity, but for its profound spiritual depth and authentic theological meaning.

Deacon Victor Beshir
October 4, 2002
Florida, USA

St. Pope Kyrillos VI blessing a married couple

Chapter One

*Introduction to the Prayers of the Holy
Matrimony, the Crowning Ceremony*

First: the Heavenly Wedding

The rituals and prayers of the wedding ceremony are an image of the heavenly wedding. Those who instituted these sacred rites and prayers intended to lift our hearts towards heaven, where God will eternally dwell in perpetual joy with His saints, and where our beloved bridegroom, Jesus Christ, has promised to prepare a place for us (Jn 14:2).

The rituals of the Crowning Ceremony—the Wedding Ceremony—are rich with replicas and representations of what will take place at the heavenly wedding, when the Church will be wed to her Savior, Jesus Christ. Therefore, attending the Holy Matrimony Ceremony is like watching a video filmed in heaven, where the scenes capture the joyous heavenly wedding.

Therefore, the rituals of the Holy Matrimony are a spiritual invitation to step into heaven and witness the heavenly wedding, so your soul delights with joy and longing for our heavenly bridegroom, the Lord Jesus Christ.

I almost feel you want to stop me, to ask for more clarification! Yes, my friend, I will pause at the Bible to show you some of the heavenly images before I take you back to the prayers of the Crowning Ceremony to show you the amazing conformity and similarity between the original and the copy... I mean between the heavenly wedding on one hand and the Crowning Ceremony on the other hand.

What is in Heaven?

Let me now tell you about what St. John witnessed in heaven and recorded for us in the Book of Revelation.

> "Let us be glad and rejoice and give Him glory, for the marriage of the Lamb[1] has come, and His wife has made herself ready." And to her it was granted to be arrayed in fine linen[2], clean and bright, for the fine linen is the righteous acts of the saints (Rev 19:7–8).

---

1   The Lamb is our Lord Jesus Christ.

2   White robes, made from fine linen are the righteousness of the saints.

Around the throne were twenty-four thrones, and on the thrones, I saw twenty-four elders sitting, clothed in white robes; and they had crowns of gold on their heads (Rev 4:4).

Now when He had taken the scroll, the four living creatures and the twenty-four elders fell down before the Lamb, each having a harp, and golden bowls full of incense, which are the prayers of the saints (Rev 5:8).

Then he said to me, "Write: 'Blessed are those who are called to the marriage supper of the Lamb!'" And he said to me, "These are the true sayings of God" (Rev 19:9).

And the Spirit and the bride[3] say, "Come!" And let him who hears say, "Come!" And let him who thirsts come. Whoever desires, let him take the water of life freely (Rev 22:17).

He who testifies to these things says, "Surely I am coming quickly." Amen. Even so, come, Lord Jesus! (Rev 22:20).

My Dear Reader, in heaven there will be a glorious wedding, where the bridegroom, our Lord Jesus

---

3   The bride is the church

Christ, will stand with His bride, the Church. There, we shall see white robes, crowns, incense, and prayers lifted before God.

These sacred images are also clearly seen in the Crowning Ceremony:

✤ The priests in their vestments[4]

✤ The censors filled with incense

✤ The bride in her white bridal dress

✤ The crowns are placed on the heads of the bride and bridegroom

Thus, the Church reminds us that this wedding is a miniature image of the Glorious Wedding of the Lamb... The Church also reminds the bride and groom of their place in heaven, and of the heavenly wedding that awaits them upon faithfully completing their mission.

Through these rites, I almost hear the Church saying to us: "What you are witnessing is a preview of the joy that awaits in heaven, when you will celebrate the heavenly wedding." Then our hearts rejoice and overflow with love, yearning and longing for our Lord Jesus, and we start to implore Him, saying: "Amen. Even so, come, Lord Jesus!" (Rev 22:20).

---

4   "The priest puts on his full liturgical attire and removes his shoes because he is about to perform a complete liturgy." Bishop Gregorius, *The Spiritual Values in the Mystery of Marriage,* in Arabic, (Cairo, Egypt: Bishopric of Higher Theological Studies, Coptic Culture, and Scientific Research), 12.

Moreover, to draw our hearts toward the heavenly wedding, the Church employs this wonderful psalm, Psalm 45. Before reading the psalm, let us see how St. Augustine (354–430) described it:

> For it is sung of the sacred Marriage ceremony; of the Bridegroom and the Bride; of the King and His people; of the Savior and those who are to be saved.... His sons are we, in that we are the "children of the Bridegroom"; and it is to us that this Psalm is addressed.[5]

But What is Psalm 45 about? It describes the heavenly Bridegroom. He is:

1. "Fairer than the sons of men" (verse 2).

2. He is God, and the Psalmist addresses Him, saying: "Your throne, O God, is forever and ever" (verse 6).

3. Lover of righteousness and detester of evil: "You love righteousness and hate wickedness" (verse 7).

The Psalm invites the bride to love her bridegroom: "Listen, O daughter, consider and incline your ear; forget your own people also, and your father's house; so, the King will greatly desire your beauty, because He is your Lord " (verses 10, 11).

---

5   St. Augustine, *Expositions on the Book of Psalms* XLV.1. (NPNF[1] 8).

The Church weaves this heartfelt appeal into a beautiful hymn, chanted with love and reverence during the Crowning Ceremony.

The psalm describes the bridal procession: "The virgins, her companions who follow her… They shall enter the King's palace" (verses 14, 15).

This radiant image is mirrored in the Crowning Ceremony, as the bride advances in procession, accompanied by two young women who stand beside her, each lifting a shining candle.

The repeated scenes, sacred words, and heartfelt prayers of Holy Matrimony elevate our souls to the joy of the heavenly wedding. O how beautiful, how glorious!

Second: the Heavenly Bridegroom

The Church wants us to remember our heavenly Bridegroom, the Lord Jesus Christ, every time we attend a wedding ceremony. She desires to draw our hearts to Him.

How does the Church Do That?

In the past, the Church used to receive the bridegroom with the Hymn *"Evlogimenoc."* This hymn was known as the "Hymn of the Groom."[6] Its text says:

---

6   Pope Gabriel the Fifth, *The order of Rituals in the fifteenth Century*, in Arabic, (Cairo, Egypt, The Franciscan Center for Oriental Studies), 131.

"Blessed is he who comes in the name of the Lord. Hosanna the Son of David… Hosanna in the highest."

They are the same words sung to Jesus upon His entry into Jerusalem. Thus, as we usher in the bridegroom, we are also ushering in with him, the heavenly Groom, our Lord Jesus Christ.[7]

After that, during the Verses of Cymbal, the deacons sing:

"Hail to… the True Bridegroom: Who united with humanity."

Also, in the psalm that is read before the Gospel:

"Which is like a bridegroom coming out of his chamber, and rejoices like a strong man to run its race" (Ps 19:5).

Therefore, the prayers of the ceremony are an invitation to remember our heavenly Bridegroom, who addresses us through Hosea the prophet, saying:

I will betroth you to Me forever; yes, I will betroth you to Me in righteousness and justice, in lovingkindness and mercy; I will betroth you to Me in faithfulness, and you shall know the Lord (Hos 2:19–20).

---

7   See Matthew 21:9 & Mark 11:9, 10.

St. Paul then emphasizes the betrothal of the human soul to Christ when he declares, "For I have betrothed you to one husband, that I may present you as a chaste virgin to Christ" (2 Cor 11:2).

Thus, the betrothal of the human soul has truly taken place, and the heavenly bridegroom of whom the virgin in the Song of Songs speaks is our Lord Jesus Christ... We, with all love, eagerly await that glorious day when we will be able to see Him face to face... the day when the Church will be wedded to the heavenly Groom, the blessed day of the Marriage of the Lamb... We pray that we may be invited to the Marriage Supper of the Lamb... that we may live with Him in the heavenly Jerusalem forever.

Whenever you see a bridegroom, remember our heavenly Bridegroom, the Lord Jesus Christ, and lift your heart in thanksgiving for His love for you.

Third: God's Blessings at the Wedding of Cana

The miracle of turning the water into wine at the wedding of Cana (Jn 2:1–11) is the first of Christ's miracles that revealed His Divinity. It is a miracle of creating good new wine that befits the new creature who has become a new creation through the birth of water and Spirit (Jn 3:3–6).

The Lord's presence and blessing of that wedding have given humankind the potential to return once again to taste "the wine of God's love" from which they were deprived after falling into sin.

In the past, God blessed marriage when He brought Eve to Adam and blessed them (Gen 2:22–24).

In the New Testament, once again, the Lord Jesus blessed marriage by His presence at the wedding of Cana. And through that wondrous miracle, He restored love, joy, and peace to married life. Therefore, during the prayers of the Crowning Ceremony, the Church repeatedly beseeches the Lord Jesus Christ to bless this wedding as He blessed the wedding at Cana of Galilee. For example:

> "O You who attended the wedding of Cana of Galilee, bless this marriage as you blessed that marriage."

> "May the blessing of the Lord, to His name be the honor, at the wedding of Cana of Galilee, settle upon you and your home, unify you in harmony, create spiritual love in your hearts, sustain your livelihood, fill your house, and grant you a long age and happy life with blessed children."

> "A pure marriage and a revered crown bless it, O our Lord Emmanuel, as You blessed the wedding at Cana of Galilee, for (...) the bridegroom and (...) the bride."

In the past, the Church used to celebrate the Divine Liturgy immediately after the Crowning Ceremony. During this Liturgy, the hymns of the Feast of the Wedding of Cana of Galilee[8] were chanted. and the Gospel chapter that talks about the miracle at the wedding in Cana of Galilee was read.[9]

St. Epiphanius, Bishop of Salamis, Cyprus (315–403) describes the presence of the Lord at the wedding in Cana of Galilee, and His turning of water into wine, as bringing into marriage a new joy resulting from that new type of wine.[10]

You may now understand why the Church repeatedly asks for "God's blessings at the wedding of Cana."

For He who turned water into wine is the One who transforms man to become a child of God... It is He who makes the newlyweds children of the kingdom, granting them the ability to taste the kingdom of God, to bask in His love, and rejoice in His presence... It is He who turns them into one body... It is He who blesses marriage and makes it an inexhaustible source of spiritual joy and heavenly peace...

---

8   See Pope Gabriel the fifth, *The order of Rituals in the fifteenth Century*, in Arabic, (Cairo, Egypt, The Franciscan Center for Oriental Studies), 142.

9   See Ibn Kabar, *The Lantern of Darkness for Clarifying Service, Second Part*, in Arabic, (Cairo, Egypt, Mina Organization for Printing, 1998), 187.

10   See William A. Jurgens, *The Faith of the Early Fathers* 2, (Collegeville, Minnesota: Liturgical Press, 1979), 72–73.

Fourth: the Name of the Lord Jesus and the Holy Trinity

When we attend the Crowning Ceremony, we notice that the Holy Spirit has placed the name of the Lord Jesus Christ and the Holy Trinity in every prayer and in every hymn. For example:

"We worship you, O Christ, with Your Good Father and the Holy Spirit, for You have come and saved us."

"The grace of God the Father be with you all."

"Glory to the Father, and to the Son, and to the Holy Spirit, now and ever and unto the ages of the ages."

"Bless your two servants, the bride and bridegroom, who are united at this hour. Grant them prosperity, wisdom, and salvation's blessings, so that they may be in all godliness and all purity united in their bodies and souls and be worthy of Your blessing and glorify Your Holy name together with Your Only Begotten Son and the Holy Spirit now and forever and unto the age of ages. Amen."

The Holy Spirit does it, so we may realize that we are in the presence of God... So, we may rest in His shadow, understand that the mystery we are witnessing is not an earthly celebration, but rather, it is a Divine work encompassing the mystery of God... Thus, our hearts get filled with reverence, and we pour out our supplications before God.

Fifth: the Symphony of Spiritual Joy

1. The Mystery of Holy Matrimony may be called the Mystery of Joy since everything within it leads to splendid spiritual joy:

✠ For union with Christ as the Bridegroom generates in the soul a joy that is "inexpressible and full of glory" (1 Pet 1:8).

✠ The Church prays for the couple that their lives may be filled with joy.

✠ In the confidence of faith, the Church perceives the joy that God will bestow upon the couple and asks them to receive this blessed joy.

2. Come, let us listen together to this beautiful symphony of joy expressed in the prayers that the Church offers on behalf of the couple during the Ceremony:

"Join Your two servants (...) and (...) ... and to enter into the law of joy."

"Grant them joy and gladness."

"Crowns of joy and happiness."

"Crowns of jubilation and delight."

3. The Church also addresses the groom, saying:

"Accept the joy and the gift of God that our God Christ grant you."

"Go with joy to your bridal chamber, which is ornamented with varied things."

The Holy Spirit invites us to understand that God is the giver of genuine gladness to the heart… He desires that the heart rejoice and be glad… We need to receive this gladness from God…

After reading these litanies, do you see the amount of joy that God will grant to the couple through the liturgy of the Holy Matrimony?

The Spirit invites the couple to discover and receive the mystery of true heavenly happiness that has been granted to them, a happiness found in the spiritual joy, next to which all worldly joy is counted as nothing.

Yet, the married couple will receive this joy when they listen to the prayers; they lift up their hearts with supplications; they stand in awe and reverence.

Now that the married couple has received this blessed gift of heavenly joy, is it necessary for them to follow it with worldly celebrations marked by impure dancing and excessive drinking to feel that their joy is complete? Will God's gift and His joy continue to thrive in their lives after such conduct? Do they not risk losing the great blessings they have just received?

"For what fellowship has righteousness with lawlessness? And what communion has light with darkness? And what accord has Christ with Belial?" (2 Cor 6:14–15).

As we watched the Crowning Ceremony, we can testify to what we have seen:

✛ During it, God pours into the couple's hearts a wonderful heavenly joy.

✛ It is a wholesome spiritual joy that fills the soul with a heavenly delight unlike anything found on earth.

✛ It is especially important not to confuse the joy of God with worldly pleasures such as dancing or drinking.

✛ The newlyweds should strive to preserve this precious treasure of joy, whose value is far greater than pearls.

Sixth: Internal Peace

In the age marked by turmoil, disagreements, disturbances, personal and social uncertainties, violence, stress, and fear and anxiety, how desperately the new home longs for the peace that God alone can bestow, a spiritual peace that is "not as the world gives" (Jn 14:27).

That is why the Church, in the prayers of the Holy Matrimony, lifts supplications, asking for this peace for the newlyweds. Listen with me to these prayers:

"Be a mediator for the groom and his helpmate, adjoin (…) and (…) through the pledge of fellowship, and grant them the sign of their union, so that, through the bond of love, they may be unified in harmony, and say unto them, 'My peace I give you both; My peace I leave with you both.' For You are the peace of us all."

"Bless and guard this wedding of Your two servants (…) and (…) in peace, harmony, and love, and protect them."

"Lengthen their lives with length of days, that they may live in meekness, calmness, endurance, and submission, and keep them blameless and without offense."

In the deacons' response, they say:

"My peace, which I have taken from My Father, I leave unto you, from now and forever."

In another litany, the Church asks for all present:

"O Christ the Logos of the Father, the only-begotten God, grant us Your peace, which is full of every joy."

Have you heard, together with me, these heartfelt pleas and supplications? They express the heart of the Church, a loving mother for her children, praying and interceding for the newlyweds, with requests that are more precious than all the treasures of the world, because the giver of these gifts is God alone. Only He can give these gifts ...

Does God answer these prayers?

Yes, He does, when they are requested from hearts that truly believe; when they rise fervently from those who love the newlyweds, those who realize that their attendance is not a mere obligation, but a responsibility towards the newlyweds, the responsibility of joining the Church in earnest prayers for the newlyweds.

Seventh: Asking for Harmony Between the Bride and Bridegroom

The Church, being a tender mother who loves her children, knows the warfare waged by the enemy and recognizes that the newlyweds need special grace to unite their hearts in love and in utmost harmony. Therefore, the Crowning Ceremony prayers are filled with many requests to God to be the source of unity, harmony, and love between the newlyweds.

It is deeply moving to witness the Church offering such fervent supplications—not only through her priests, but through every member of the congregation. How beautiful it is when all hearts rise together in love and prayer for the newlyweds, entrusting their union to God.

Beloved brothers and sisters, when you are invited to a Crowning Ceremony, lift your hearts in sincere prayer for the newly formed family. I kindly ask you to put aside small talk and casual comments during the ceremony, and let your heart enter into a spirit of quiet, prayerful reverence. The future of this family is precious and deserves our heartfelt, earnest prayers before God.

Now, come, let us see: How does the Church ask for harmony and unity between the bride and the groom? The Church presents these sacred supplications:

> "Be a mediator for the groom and his helpmate, adjoin (...) and (...) through the pledge of fellowship, and grant them the sign of their union, so that, through the bond of love, they may be unified in harmony."

The Church here asks God to be the mediator and the weaver of the threads of intimacy between the newlyweds and the one who holds the bond of love between them.

This is the difference between a Christian marriage and any other marriage: Christian marriage is a work of God's grace, a hidden mystery of God that works in secret to unite the two into one. It is a sacred bond that becomes stronger and more cohesive with the passage of time, unlike many earthly marriages that begin with great excitement yet weaken with time.

Here are other examples of the Church prayers for the bride and bridegroom:

> "Bless the union of Your two servants (...) and (...) who are united to each other according to Your will."

"Confirm their union."

Such supplications continue as we stand in reverent awe, listening to the beautiful hymns and wondering about what has happened. Then comes the answer:

When the Church looked with the eye of faith, she saw this great multitude of her children, those who have attained the Mystery of Holy Matrimony, and those who will one day seek it. She saw those who, during the ceremony, opened their hearts to the Holy Spirit in earnest prayer, asking earnestly.

And the Holy Spirit came and created harmony, affection, love, and understanding between the newlyweds. And both became like musical instruments with tuned strings, producing to the ear the most beautiful melodies of love, unity, and harmony.

The Church sees this divine work and sings this glorious hymn:

"Those whom the Holy Spirit has attuned together, as a stringed instrument, always blessing God."

O blessed groom and blessed bride, how I wish with all my heart that you pray and ask for this harmony, and how I hope that you will attain it through these prayers, and be as keen on preserving it as you would be on preserving a precious treasure?

Chapter Two

What Takes Place During the Crowning Ceremony?

The Bridal Procession into the Church

The Bridal procession enters the Church, preceded by:

First, the Deacons

They chant the joyous Hymn "O King of Peace." This hymn indicates that the procession includes not only the bride and the bridegroom but also the Lord Jesus Christ, the King of Peace. The Lord Jesus Christ is present because He is the first partner in this spiritual marriage… For in the Orthodox teaching, marriage is the union between two in the third: A union between the bride and groom in Christ. The bride and groom are members of the body of Christ, the Church. They are both united in Christ.

On this sacred and spiritual occasion, they surrender themselves and their lives to the heavenly Groom. The bride, a member of the Church, the Bride of Christ, offers her life to the heavenly Bridegroom… And here in this marriage, she also presents herself as a bride to her groom.

Second, the Priests

Priests as God's servants and stewards of His mysteries; we see them walking in this procession, dressed in their priestly vestments.

Third, the Groom and the Bride

The bride walks to the right of the groom, which is her place from this time on, signifying acceptance, love, appreciation, and respect.

The procession then is a holy procession, composed of Christ, the clergy—stewards of His mysteries—, and His servants, the deacons. It is the entrance procession into the kingdom of Christ,[11] where the newlyweds will be united in Christ. The procession reminds us of this joyful spectacle in which all nations, all tribes, and all peoples will attend the wedding of the bride (the Church) to her heavenly Bridegroom.

The Beginning of the Prayers of Holy Matrimony

Everyone heads towards the Holy Altar, where a Holy Mystery of the Church will be completed, the Liturgy of

---

11   See John Meyendorff, *Marriage, An Orthodox Perspective*, (New York, NY: St. Vladimir's Seminary Press, 1984), 34.

the Holy Matrimony, where all these holy acts take place:

✠ The Holy Spirit descends to unite the newlyweds.

✠ They are anointing with holy oil.

✠ Holy crowns are placed upon them, and priestly vestments are worn.

✠ Incense, litanies (prayers), and church hymns are offered.

✠ And above all, the Lord Jesus Himself is present as a partner in this marriage. And present with Him are His holy angels and His saints.

Indeed, how awesome and great this mystery is! How wonderful is God's miraculous work in it!

In his profound pastoral reflection on Ephesians 5, John Chrysostom teaches that Christian marriage is not merely a partnership or association, but a mysterious transformation brought about by God Himself. Through marriage, the two are united so completely that their former separateness is overcome, and they are joined into a single, living unity. Thus, Chrysostom declares:

"After marriage, you are no longer two, but have become one flesh. You have become one [person], one living creature."[12]

---

12   Chrysostom, John, *Homilies on the Epistle to the Ephesians*, Homily 20 (on Ephesians 5:22–33), in *Nicene and Post-Nicene Fathers*, First Series, vol. 13. Copeland W. J., trans.; Schaff P., ed. (Rapids, MI: Eerdmans, Grand, 1989), 146.

As for Tertullian (160–220 AD), he says:

How beautiful, then, the marriage of two Christians, two who are one in hope, one in desire, one way of life they follow… They are both children of one Father and servants of the same Master; no division of spirit or flesh; no, they are truly two in one flesh. Where there is one flesh, there is also one spirit.[13]

The Bride Sits to the Right of the Groom

This solemn procession stops near the altar, where two seats are placed for the bride and groom, in the south of the church, in front of the sanctuary. The priests and deacons stand opposite them.

Why does the bride sit to the right of the groom?

This image is identical to the heavenly wedding as pictured in Psalm 45: "Kings' daughters are among Your honorable women; at Your right hand stands the queen in gold from Ophir" (Ps 45:9).

Inspired by the Holy Spirit, the Church draws our attention to the heavenly wedding even from the first moments of the Holy Matrimony Prayers.

Standing next to the newlyweds are two young women, each holding a beautiful, tall candle. Why?

13   Tertullian, *Ad Uxorem* (To His Wife). The *Ante-Nicene Fathers*, vol. 4, Thelwall S., trans. Roberts A. and Donaldson J., eds. (Grand Rapids, MI: Eerdmans, 1989), 45–46.

Going back to Psalm 45, the Church's Wedding Psalm, we find it says: "The virgins, her companions who follow her, shall be brought to You" (Ps 45:14).

In some other Orthodox churches, we see that each of the bride and groom is given a candle to hold throughout the wedding prayers. But why?

They say that the wedding prayers remind us of the heavenly wedding. And the Lord Christ has likened the Kingdom of Heaven to a wedding more than once. In one of them, He said:

> Then the kingdom of heaven shall be likened to ten virgins who took their lamps and went out to meet the bridegroom. Now five of them were wise.... The wise took oil in their vessels with their lamps.... at midnight a cry was heard: "Behold, the bridegroom is coming...." Then all those virgins arose and trimmed their lamps (Mt 25:1–13).

Therefore, this parable talks about receiving the heavenly Bridegroom, the Lord Jesus, with lamps full of oil, to give light and illumination. Likewise, in the wedding, the newlyweds hold the shining candles, declaring their longing for the heavenly Bridegroom, their readiness to receive Him, to enter into His Kingdom, to offer their lives to Him, to be united with Him, and to live in His fear to have the share of the wise virgins.

This ritual shows us that all the Orthodox Churches agree that the Holy Matrimony prayer is a microcosm of the celebration of the heavenly wedding and a spiritual entrance into it. We live it with heart, thought and longing; by self-preparation and spiritual readiness.

Blessings of the Wedding Rings

The priest ties the two rings with a red ribbon[14] (called Zennar) and holds them in his hand while declaring the union of the bride and bridegroom three times:

"In the name of our Lord, God, and Savior Jesus Christ, the founder of the statute of perfection and the author of the law of graces, we declare in this Orthodox assembly and before the altar of the Lord of hosts the union of possession and the marriage of the blessed Orthodox son (...) to his betrothed, the blessed Orthodox daughter (...)."

---

14   In the past, the two rings along with the two crowns used to be tied together and bundled with a rectangular piece of white cloth while blessed three times with the cross because the wedding ceremony does not get performed with the rings alone. Please review: Bishop Gregorius, *The Spiritual Values in the Mystery of Marriage*, in Arabic; (Cairo, Egypt: Bishopric of Higher Theological Studies, Coptic Culture, and Scientific Research), 13–14; Father Yoohanna Salama, *The Precious Pearls of the Church Rituals*, Part Two, in Arabic, (Cairo, Egypt: St. George Bookstore), 121; Hegumen Mankerious Awadallah, *Minaret of the Holiness*, the Fifth book, in Arabic, (Cairo, Egypt), 139.

He signs the rings in the name of the Father, followed by the congregations saying, "Amen," and "Our Father who art in heaven."

"In the name of our Lord, God, and Savior Jesus Christ, the founder of the statute of perfection and the author of the law of graces, we declare in this Orthodox assembly and before the altar of the Lord of hosts the union of possession and the marriage of the blessed Orthodox daughter (...) to her betrothed, the blessed Orthodox son (...)."

He signs the rings in the name of the Son, followed by the congregations saying, "Amen," and "Our Father who art in heaven."

"In the name of our Lord, God, and Savior Jesus Christ, the founder of the statute of perfection and the author of the law of graces, we declare in this Orthodox assembly and before the altar of the Lord of hosts the union of possession and the marriage of the blessed Orthodox son (…) to his betrothed, the blessed Orthodox daughter (…)."

He signs the rings in the name of the Holy Spirit, after which the congregation responds with "Amen," and "Our Father who art in heaven."

So, the priest announces to everyone that this marriage takes place in the name of the Lord Jesus, in His presence, and before the altar of the Lord of hosts.

How full of awe is this! And how sacred! We are witnessing a marriage contract to be completed in the name of God, His strength, and His grace. It is a spiritual marriage.

The two rings are blessed in the name of the Father, the Son, and the Holy Spirit. Blessing the rings with the sign of the cross and in the name of the Father, the Son, and the Holy Spirit at the beginning of the prayers is an invocation of the Holy Trinity to attend and unite the couple. Therefore, these are glorious moments that must be witnessed in reverence and supplication. It requires all those present to pray earnestly to God to unite the newlyweds and establish a new church in their home.

These are moments of prayer and reverence that call everyone to add their voices, not their cheers, to the voice of the deacons as they pray: Amen… Amen… Amen!

This calls for focusing attention on prayers, reverence, and respect for the mystery being performed by refraining from talking and by avoiding distractions, such as taking photos that draw attention away from prayer.

The priest then prays the Prayer of Thanksgiving It is the custom of the Church to begin all her prayers with "the Prayer of Thanksgiving," in which the priest offers thanks to God for everything, concerning everything, and in everything.

Following the Prayer of Thanksgiving, the deacons sing the Verses of the Cymbals, including the following verse:

"Hail to the bridal chamber that is adorned with all types, for the true Bridegroom, who united with humanity."

Thus, from the very beginning, the Church raises her eyes to see the Lord Jesus Christ, the true Bridegroom who united Himself with us so that we may be one in Him.

Then the priest prays, asking God to be a mediator for the newlyweds, and to bind them with the bond of love and to grant them His peace.

Blessing of the Vestments

Now, let's return together to follow the rites of the Mystery of Holy Matrimony and discover the spiritual treasures and blessings within it. We will notice that the priest prays over a golden vestment (cloak), which he then places on the groom.

What are These Vestments, and Why are They Placed on the Groom?

To answer this question, we need to pause and reflect on the story of the Wedding Garment. Do you remember, my dear reader, the parable of the Wedding Feast recorded in Matthew 22:2–14? The parable tells us that when the king came in to see the guests, he noticed a man who was not wearing a wedding garment. The king then said to the servants, "Bind him hand and foot, take him away, and cast him into outer darkness."

St. Clement of Alexandria (150–220), commenting on this parable, writes:

Here is the preparation for the wedding to which we are invited. The person who has prepared himself will say, "Now my joy will be fulfilled." As for the unwise and unprepared man will hear the words of the Lord, "Friend, how did you come in here without a wedding garment?"[15]

So, the Lord asks us to prepare for the heavenly wedding by putting on the Wedding Garment on that day... And the Church, in her holy rite, wants to lift our eyes to the heavenly wedding, so she brings the vestment and prays over it, then the priest puts it on the groom.

St. Jerome (342–420) relates these garments to the Parable of the Wedding Feast, saying, "The wedding garments are the Lord's commands and the works that are fulfilled from the Law and the Gospel. These become the clothing of the new man."[16]

It is as though the Church is saying: "Behold, O bridegroom, you are now clothed in the garments that remind you of the garment of the heavenly wedding, so that you may strive to enter the Kingdom of Heaven, preparing yourself and your household for the day of the 'Lamb's Wedding.'"

---

15   Clement of Alexandria, *The Instructor (Paedagogus)*. In *Ante-Nicene Fathers* 2, Wilson W., trans.; Roberts A. and Donaldson J., eds. (Grand Rapids, MI: Eerdmans, 1885), 254.

16   St. Jerome, *Commentary on Matthew*, Scheck T.P., trans. (Washington, D.C.: Catholic University of America Press, 2008), 250.

But What does the Church Say in Her Prayers over These Garments?

"We ask you, Good One, the Lover of Mankind, bless these vestments."

"Vestments of glory and salvation."

"Vestments of joy and delight."

"Preserve them both pure in soul, body, and spirit."

These garments, therefore, become a source of spiritual grace that aids in salvation. They bring joy and delight, and they lead to glory.

While the priest arrays the groom with this vestment, the deacons chant:

"The spiritual raiment covers Michael, and the girdle of jewels Michael has put on. The raiment of chastity has been given to this bridegroom, and the crown of joy, has been placed upon his head."

The Church has captivated our thoughts towards heaven and put us before the scene of the "wedding of the Lamb (Christ)" to see Archangel Michael robed in the spiritual garment in full preparation for the heavenly wedding. Then she brings us back to see the groom dressed in the garment of chastity.

How do you feel, my dear reader, when you see the Church giving your brother, the bridegroom, the garment of chastity? Should you not say from the depths of your heart: Amen, Amen, Amen? Would you also not earnestly pray for yourself and for all your loved ones that on the last day you would be ready and dressed in wedding garments?

My dear bridegroom, you have put on a holy garment, the garment of chastity, to strive, as a good soldier of Christ, to gain eternity, and to abandon the love of the world and the attachment to sin, and to offer your heart and your life wholly to God.

But you may ask: The prayers say:

"Bless these vestments, so that they become for Your two servants who will wear them, through the pleasure of Your goodness, vestments of glory and salvation. Amen.

"Vestments of joy and delight. Amen.

"Preserve them both pure in soul, body, and spirit. Amen."

Thus, the prayer appears to refer to the garments of both the bride and groom. So, where is the garment of the bride?

Where is the Bride's Garment?

Yes, in the past, the Church used to pray over the robes

of both the groom and the bride.[17] In this prayer, the priest asks God to bless them as His servants, the groom and the bride.

The litany clearly says:

"So that they become for Your two servants who will wear them, through the pleasure of Your goodness."

Therefore, it is clear from the ceremony and its prayers that there used to be a garment (a robe) for the bride. This practice stopped over the years, but the good news is that it has been revived. This is crucial as both the bride and the bridegroom need this sacred blessing.

17   Father Yoohanna Salama, *The Precious Pearls of the Church Rituals*, Part Two, in Arabic, (Cairo, Egypt: St. George Bookstore), 134.

The Two Gold Wedding Rings

At the beginning of the prayers, the priest placed the two gold wedding rings on a red silk ribbon and blessed them three times with the sign of the cross. The wedding rings were then placed on the couple's fingers. Now the question is:

Why Two Wedding Rings, and Why Gold?

St. Clement of Alexandria (150–220 AD) associated the use of rings with entrusted responsibility, dignity, and honorable stewardship when he writes: "Let a signet ring be worn… for a seal is needed."[18]

This statement shows that the purpose of a ring in Christian life is not vanity, but meaningful symbolism. This understanding is reflected in the use of rings in Christian marriage, since a wedding is founded upon trust, dignity, fidelity, and honor.

The words of St. Clement of Alexandria also echo the Lord's declaration in the book of Haggai: "'I will make you like a signet ring; for I have chosen you,' says the Lord of hosts" (Hag 2:23).

In the same way, the ring given by the bridegroom to his bride signifies the honor, love, and dignity she receives in this sacred union, just as God honored Zerubbabel by calling him His signet ring.

---

18   Clement of Alexandria, *The Instructor (Paedagogus).* In *Ante-Nicene Fathers* 2, Wilson W., trans.; Roberts A. and Donaldson J., eds. (Grand Rapids, MI: Eerdmans, 1885), 285.

Tertullian (155–240 AD) recognized the betrothal ring as part of the marriage process.[19]

What does the Holy Bible Say About the Ring?

Joseph received Pharaoh's signet ring (Gen 41:42) to state that he had attained the highest rank in Egypt and that he had won the trust of Pharaoh.

In the parable of the prodigal son, when the son returned, the father commanded that a ring be put on his finger (Lk 15:22), a sign of acceptance and trust.

Therefore, each spouse's name is engraved on the ring worn by the other. The giving of the rings becomes a sign that the groom has given himself entirely to the bride, and she has likewise given herself entirely to him. Each now belongs to the other, and each is lovingly bound to the other.

Moreover, the ring is a token of love and a sign of the covenant that binds them together, for he gave her his ring, and she gave him her ring. This also means accepting the one other as they are, with their strengths and shortcomings, and that each complements the other's shortcomings.[20]

---

19   See Tertullian: *Treatises on Marriage and Remarriage*, W.P. Le Saint, trans. (New York: Newman Press, 1951). 46–47.
20   John Meyendorff, *Marriage, An Orthodox Perspective*. (NY, Vladimir Seminary Press, 1975), 32.

Why Gold?

Gold is used in the Crowning Ceremony to indicate the great value and privilege of the marital bond because gold is the most precious, pure, and beautiful metal.

Gold does not rust and does not deteriorate with the passage of time; it is unaffected by changing environmental conditions. Therefore, it is the best analogy for the loving relationship that binds a husband and his wife. This relationship does not weaken or change despite changes in economic, health, or social circumstances.

Early Christian Wedding Rings: Discovery, Meaning, and Devotion

The archaeological discovery of Early Christian and Byzantine rings in the Zucker Family Collection offers a compelling glimpse into the spiritual lives of early believers, of the first generations of believers. Carefully studied by art historian Gary Vikan,[21] these rings, dating from the third to the seventh century, reveal how early Christians adopted the Roman custom of exchanging rings and transformed it into a symbol of spiritual commitment. Engraved with crosses, Christograms, clasped hands, doves, and even images of Christ blessing a bride and groom, these rings testify that Christian

---

21   Vikan G. "Early Christian and Byzantine Rings in the Zucker Family Collection." *The Journal of the Walters Art Gallery* 45 (1987): 32–43.

marriage was understood not merely as a legal contract but as a covenant rooted in divine grace.

Some rings bear the inscription *omonoia* ("concord"), expressing marital unity in Christ. Others depict the couple standing beneath the blessing hand of Christ, visually proclaiming that their union is sanctified "in the Lord." These artifacts connect textual sources like Clement of Alexandria and Tertullian with the tangible expression of faith worn daily by Christian couples. The rings demonstrate that Christians have infused marriage symbols with spiritual meaning from the earliest centuries.

Beyond their historical and artistic value, these rings speak to the heart. In a hostile world, early Christians marked their marriages with signs of Christ's presence. Their rings were quiet prayers made visible. The clasped hands engraved on gold, the tiny crosscut into gold, the image of Christ stretching out His hand in blessing, each of these details reveals a couple who desired their love to be shaped by the Gospel. Their homes, like their rings, were meant to be small sanctuaries where the love of God took root in daily life.

When we look upon these ancient rings, we see more than archaeological artifacts. We see the faith of husbands and wives who believe that marriage is a path to holiness. We notice the continuity of Christian love across centuries. We are invited to remember that the symbols we use today are part of a long tradition practiced by believers who entrusted their union to God. The early Christians who once wore these rings walked hand in hand in fidelity toward the Kingdom, encircled by a sign that pointed beyond themselves to the eternal love of Christ.

Why the Red Ribbon?

Silk is an expensive fabric that is both durable and soft, just like Christian marriage, which is a precious and strong bond, enveloped in love, tenderness, empathy, and gentle affection.

The red color refers to the blood of our Lord Jesus Christ:

"To Him who loved us and washed us from our sins in His own blood" (Rev 1:5).

"Redeemed us to God by Your blood" (Rev 5:9).

"Knowing that you were not redeemed with corruptible things, like silver or gold... but with the precious blood of Christ, as of a lamb without blemish and without spot" (1 Pet 1:18–19).

In the past, Rahab put a scarlet thread (red in color) on her house, for her and everyone in her household to have salvation and life (Josh 2:18–19). Many Fathers have said that the scarlet thread that Rahab used is a reference to the salvation accomplished by the blood of Christ.[22]

---

22   See St. Ambrose, *On Christian Faith*, 5, 10, St. Justin Martyr,

St. Clement of Rome (92–101) comments on Rahab's act (Josh 2:18), saying:

And they gave her a sign that she should hang out from her house a scarlet thread, thereby making it clear that through the blood of the Lord redemption will come to all who believe and hope in God.[23]

Therefore, the red ribbon reminds us of the salvation that took place on the cross. It is a precious salvation brimming with the Savior's love, His abundant feelings for humanity, and His constant willingness to wash us from our sins with His holy blood.

We have seen that the two rings were tied with this silk ribbon:

✤ This is a sign that the bond uniting husband and wife is also bound with the Lord Jesus Christ, our Savior. He is the beloved Bridegroom who redeemed us with His precious blood.

✤ It is an indication that the Savior's love will reign over their hearts and that salvation is the ultimate goal in the life of the newlyweds.

Dialogue with Trypho, 111 & St. Irenaeus, *Adv. Her.*, IV.20.
23   Clement of Rome. *The First Epistle of Clement to the Corinthians*, Ehrman B.D., trans. In *The Apostolic Fathers*, Volume I, edited by Bart D. Ehrman, (Cambridge, Massachusetts: Harvard University Press, 2003), 48.

The Bridegroom and the Red Ribbon

We will observe that the priest places a red ribbon around the bridegroom's chest and back, resting it on his shoulder. What does this mean?

The red ribbon symbolizes the salvation offered by the Lord on the cross. Therefore, when the groom carries the ribbon on his shoulder, it is an indication that he carries salvation and its blessings, leading his family toward the path of salvation. It is also a reference to carrying the cross in spiritual warfare against sin, Satan, and the world.

Crowning Ceremony and the
Blessed Virgin Mary

Then we see the priest holding a censor from which pillars of sweet, scented incense rise, carrying our prayers and supplications.

Now listen carefully, and you will hear the deacons chanting the beautiful hymn of *Tai Shorey* (This Censor), which likens the censor to the Blessed Virgin Mary.

> *But why invoke the Blessed Virgin Mary in a wedding setting?*

Throughout history, many women dedicated their lives to Christ and were truly Christ's brides; yet the Virgin Mary surpassed them all. She stands as the true exemplar of the bride of Christ. This is why the Church praises the Virgin Mary in the Crowning Ceremony, for she is the ultimate bride.

Here are some occasions during which the Blessed Virgin Mary is praised in the Church:

In Wednesday's Theotokia:[24]

"The Father looked from heaven and found no one like you. He sent His only begotten Son, who came and took flesh from you."

In the "Hail to Mary the Queen":

"Hail to Mary the Queen... You have found Grace, O bride. Let us honor the virginity of the bride without blemish: the pure, the all-holy, the Mother of God, Mary."

In Sunday's Theotokia:

---

24   Theotokias are hymns of praise for St. Mary. The word Theotokia is derived from "Theotokos," which means "Mother of God."

"He was incarnate, of the Holy Spirit, and of Mary, the pure Bride."

And in the communion hymn during the feasts and fast of the Virgin Mary:

"For the Lord who is without beginning chose you as a throne for Him, O wondrous bride, O Mary, the daughter of Joachim."

Because St. Mary is the perfect example of the Bride of Christ, the Church puts the Virgin Mary in the Crowning Ceremony's prayers from beginning to end in an amazing way that led one author to say:

The service of the Mystery of Marriage in the Coptic rite—from its beginning to its end—draws our hearts toward Saint Mary as the bride, as if inviting us to prepare ourselves to become the eternal bride of Christ.[25]

Come now, let us follow what the church proclaims about the Virgin Mary in the Crowning Ceremony, and why?

Because the purpose of the wedding prayer is to direct our attention to the heavenly wedding ceremony that will take place between the Bridegroom, the Lord of Glory, and His bride, the Church, whose perfect example is the Virgin Mary, we therefore find many

---

25   Hegumen Tadros Yacob Malaty, *Saint Mary in the Orthodox Concept*, in Arabic, (Alexandria, Egypt: St. George Coptic Orthodox Chrich, Sporting, 1978), 69.

hymns that speak of the heavenly Bridegroom and His beloved Bride. For example:

1. At the beginning of the Crowning Ceremony, a magnificent scene unfolds:

In the old rite, the Church first received the groom. He entered the church in a glorious procession while the deacons chanted the groom's hymn *Evlogimenos*, thus ushering in the heavenly Bridegroom with the groom.

Then the priests and deacons return to receive the bride, with the hymn "Hail to Mary the Queen," as a reminder of the bride in the heavenly wedding.

There are three prayers in the Crowning Ceremony, and at the end of each one, there is a litany of praise for the Virgin Mary.

2. Before reading the Pauline epistle, the deacons sing "*Tai Shori*," a hymn for the Virgin Mary.

3. In the old rite, they used to sing a hymn called "Praise to the True Bride, the Mother of God," which includes the following:

"Come and behold this bride, robed in great glory, whom the Lamb loved. John, Son of Zebedee, Son of Thunder, says, 'This bride is more luminous than the morning star. This is the New Zion, the city of our God. The joy of all the saints is in her.'"[26]

---

26   Ibn Kebar, *The Lantern of Darkness for Clarifying Service,*

You may have noticed the beautiful connection indicated in the Coptic rite. Although the apostle John speaks of the Bride of the Lamb in this hymn, the rite refers to it as "Praise of the True Bride, the Mother of God," as if the Church wants us to say: This bride is the Church, and the Virgin Mary is her perfect example of the bride. Therefore, she was worthy to bear the Son in the incarnation.

The ceremony is concluded with the hymn "Hail to Mary the Queen."

Back in History

As mentioned before, our ancient Coptic manuscripts describe the ritual of matrimony, saying:

"The church used to receive the bridegroom first with the hymn of the Bridegroom, thus ushering the heavenly bridegroom with him.

"This is immediately followed by the reception of the bride with the hymn of 'Hail to Mary the Queen,' so we receive the Bride of Christ, represented by the Virgin Mary."

The excellence and authenticity of the Crowning Ceremony rituals are revealed in the way it puts the heavenly wedding before our eyes from the beginning. At present, the couple are ushered in together with the

Second Part, in Arabic, (Cairo, Egypt, Mina Organization for Printing, 1998), p. 184. Thanks to the late Fr. Kyrillos Makar for translating this hymn from the original Coptic text.

"King of Peace" hymn and ushered out with the hymn "Hail to Mary the Queen."

⁓

The deacon then reads from St. Paul's Epistle to the Ephesians 5:22–6:3. You may ask: What is the point of the biblical readings in the crowning ceremony?

The Church always reads from the Holy Bible in all her services, because there is an important ecclesiastical principle that teaches that everything is sanctified by both the word of God and prayers, as it is written: "For it is sanctified by the word of God and prayer" (1 Tim 4:5).

In addition, the word of God is alive and powerful,[27] and it sanctifies and cleanses.[28] The readings are also instructive. The Church chooses the readings that are suitable for teaching in all its numerous services.[29] Here you may ask:

What instruction is in the part of the epistle that the Church reads in the Crowning Ceremony?

✤ It contains an explanation of the holy union that takes place in the Mystery of Matrimony, which reflects the union of Christ with the Church.

✤ It presents a beautiful and comprehensive summary of the relationship of newlyweds.

---

27   See Heb 4:12.
28   See Eph 5:26.
29   See Eph 5:22–33.

✤ Here, the Church lays before them a "constitution" for their married life that arranges their relationship, and sets before them the relationship between Christ and the Church as a model to follow:

✤ "Husbands, love your wives, just as Christ also loved the church and gave Himself for her,"

✤ "Wives, submit to your own husbands, as to the Lord."

✤ "For the husband is head of the wife, as also Christ is head of the church."

Here are some words of the Epistle to Ephesians read by the deacon:

✤ "So, husbands ought to love their own wives as their own bodies; he who loves his wife loves himself."

✤ "For this reason, a man shall leave his father and mother and be joined to his wife, and the two shall become one flesh."

✤ "This is a great mystery."

✤ "And let the wife see that she respects her husband."

The above verses do not imply inequality between men and women. The Bible affirms the equality of both sexes, as stated, "There is neither male nor female; for you are all one in Christ Jesus" (Gal 3:28).

Do you notice the greatness of these words?

Would you not agree that if the bride and groom truly listen to these words and allow them to guide their relationship, their marriage would become a source of joy, happiness, and blessing for them?

I wish all those present in the church would also listen attentively to these golden words, for they hold the golden key to the house of joy, peace, and happiness.

The Lord made the laws of marriage clear in the Bible:

✤ The deacons might sing the hymn "*Pi Epnevma*"[30] which is the hymn of the descent of the Holy Spirit.

✤ Then the Trisagion hymn ("Holy God, Holy Mighty, Holy Immortal") is chanted. The Church reminds us that when the prophet Isaiah heard the angelic cry, "Holy, Holy, Holy" (Isaiah 6:3,4), the gates of heaven were shaken. So we are called to stand in awe and reverence before God.

✤ This is followed by the priest praying the litany of the Gospel, after which the Gospel is read from: Matthew 19:1–6.

In this biblical reading, the Lord institutes the marriage laws clearly:

1. "He who made them at the beginning made them male and female."

30　This hymn is not found in the old books of the Crowning Ceremony rituals.

2. "For this reason a man shall leave his father and mother and be joined to his wife, and the two shall become one flesh? So then, they are no longer two but one flesh." Then it addresses the mystic way that unifies the two, making them one.

3. "Therefore, what God has joined together, let not man separate." This means it is neither within anyone's right nor under anyone's authority to separate the two whom God has joined together.

4. The Lord also says, "And I say to you, whoever divorces his wife, except for sexual immorality, and marries another, commits adultery" (Mt 19:9).

Then the litanies are prayed, which include supplications to God to:

"Bless this marriage… hear us and have mercy on us."

How beautiful is the depth of our Church's rituals! For, although we are amid the joy of the Holy Matrimony, the Church does not forget to supplicate and ask for repentance and mercy.

In this litany, the priest asks twelve times with the supplication:

"We ask you, O Lord, to hear us and have mercy upon us." Or "We beseech You to hear us and have mercy on us."

And the people repeat: "Lord have mercy."

That is a great spiritual lesson. It includes: A call to those who are distracted with conversation to lift up their hearts in supplication, repeating "Lord have mercy"; a reminder to concentrate on the prayers more than on taking pictures or distributing gifts and candy during the ceremony.

This is followed by "The Three Short Litanies." These are prayers for the peace of the Church, the patriarch, the bishops, and the Church assemblies.

The people then recite the Creed and chant the last part: "We look for the resurrection of the dead and the life of the age to come, Amen."

Then the three matrimonial prayers are prayed.

What is the content of these three matrimonial prayers?

The First Prayer

It addresses God who created both man and woman and who said that it is not good for man to be alone. Then it asks:

"Join your two servants (...) and (...) to be united to each other in one body."

Thus, the Church asks God to grant them to become one body.

The deacons repeat a hymn for peace and praise the blessed Virgin Mary:

"The gate of the east is Mary the Virgin, the chaste bridal chamber, for the pure bridegroom."

The Second Prayer

It asks God to bless the couple as He blessed the forefathers in the Old Testament, for example, Abraham and Sara, and Isaac and Rebecca. Thus, the Church prays that the same blessing be bestowed upon the couple so that they may become a living part of the victorious Church.

The deacons then chant a hymn in which Christ promises the continuity of peace. It also has a praise for the Blessed Virgin Mary:

"My peace which I have taken from My Father, I leave unto you, from now and forever."

"All the kings of the earth walk in your light, and the nations in your brightness, O Mary, the Mother of God."

The Third Prayer

It addresses in detail the creation of Adam and Eve and prays for the couple, asking God to:

"Confirm their unity, guard their bed in purity. Cover them and their home with Your unconquerable Right Hand."

"Deliver them from all envy and intrigues. Preserve them in oneness, harmony, and peace, grant them joy and gladness."

"Bless them, O God, as You blessed Abraham with Sarah, and Isaac with Rebecca, and Jacob in his marriage."

Then the deacons chant a hymn reminding God of His covenant with our fathers Abraham, Isaac, and Jacob:

"Do not forget the covenant that You have established with our fathers: Abraham, Isaac, and Jacob, Israel Your saint."

Then they praise the blessed Virgin Mary, saying:

"You are brighter than the sun; you are she who is towards the east, for whom the righteous await with joy and praise."

Now, do you know why the Fathers call the Crowning Ceremony prayers the Liturgy of Crowning?

Why is It a Liturgy?

It is a liturgy because:

It sanctifies the couple.

In it, the Holy Spirit dwells in the couple.

In it, there are sanctifying prayers for the robes and the crowns.

In it, there is oil sanctification to impart to it special spiritual benefits.

In it, there are blessings of the cross.

The priest and deacons wear the special liturgical vestments and garments.

In it, there is incense and biblical readings.

In it, there are litanies, kneeling, and absolutions.

People of Christ, please come to the liturgy of the Crowning Ceremony dressed in attire appropriate to the holiness of the prayers, and stand in awe and worship, as is fitting for the sacred liturgy...

Take part in the prayers and supplications just as you would do during the Divine liturgy...

God will graciously regard your reverence, hear your prayers, and send His Holy Spirit to act powerfully in the life of the couple.

In this way, we would restore to the Coptic Crowning Ceremony its power, unity, and splendor, and we would help the couple stand steadfast in the face of life's trials.

The priest then brings a holy oil and prays over it. Thus, the Church recalls the words of Scripture: "Therefore God, Your God, has anointed You With the oil of gladness more than Your companions" (Ps 45:7).

Why does the Priest Anoint the Couple with Holy Oil?

Oil refers to the spiritual joy obtained through the Crowning Ceremony.

Oil refers to the grace of God that sanctifies their unity and shrouds them with spiritual beauty.

According to the psalm, "You anoint my head with oil; my cup runs over" (Ps 23:5).

In addition, the Church prays asking God to:

"Bless this oil with blessings, so that it becomes an oil to sanctify Your two servants (…) and (…). A weapon of righteousness and justice. Anointment of purity and incorruption. Light and unfading beauty. Joy, ornament, and true comfort. Power, salvation, and victory over the deeds of the adversary. Renewal and salvation for their souls, bodies, and spirits. Richness with the fruit of good deeds."

Dear congregation, raise your hearts in prayer, so that God may grant the couple these blessings.

At the end of these litanies, the priest anoints the bridegroom while the deacons chant:

"May this oil destroy the demons. This oil is against the evil spirits. This is the oil of holy spirits. This oil is against the impure spirits, through Jesus Christ, the King of Glory."

Then the priest anoints the bride while the deacons chant:

"You have anointed my head with oil, and Your cup cheers me like the best wine; Your mercy will follow me all the days of my life."

Dear couple, meditate upon the blessings hidden in this oil and value the great blessings present in it:

It is the beginning of joy and happiness in your life…

It is a power for salvation and renewal…

It is a weapon in your fight against sin and evil.

That is why it is particularly important to respond in your hearts to each litany, saying, "Amen."

And when the priest anoints your heads and hands, raise a thanksgiving prayer and glorification to the One who has given you all these bountiful blessings.

The Crowns

*What are Crowns? What do They
Mean in the Light of the Holy Bible?*

Crowns were once given as a reward for great achievements. St. Paul compares the earthly crown granted after winning a race to a heavenly crown:

And everyone who competes for the prize is temperate in all things. Now they do it to obtain a perishable crown, but we for an imperishable crown (1 Cor 9:25).

A Crown is a Reward for Spiritual Struggle

After a life full of spiritual efforts, St. Paul looked with an eye of faith to God's reward and said:

I have fought the good fight, I have finished the race, I have kept the faith. Finally, there is laid up for me the crown of righteousness, which the Lord, the righteous Judge, will give to me on that Day, and not to me only but also to all who have loved His appearing (2 Timothy 4:7,8).

St. Peter confirms the same truth, saying, "And when the Chief Shepherd appears, you will receive the crown of glory that does not fade away" (1 Peter 5:4).

The book of Revelation puts the same conditions for receiving the crown:

Do not fear any of those things which you are about to suffer. Indeed, the devil is about to throw some of you into prison, that you may be tested, and you will have tribulation ten days. Be faithful until death, and I will give you the crown of life (Rev 2:10).

Why does the Church Place Crowns on the Couple's Heads?

Alexander Schmemann answered this question, saying,

The Church restores marriage to its original form, not as a simple natural institution but as a sacrament of the Kingdom... the crowns are crowns of the Kingdom, of the glory and honor with which man was endowed in the beginning.[31]

St. John Chrysostom (347–407) in Homily 12 on Ephesians says, "They (the bride and groom) are crowned as if they had won the victory, because they have kept their virginity and come together in marriage in purity."[32]

In addition, the Church wants to lift our eyes to the heavenly wedding where we see the bride (the Church), and the bridegroom crowned. As said in the book of the Songs of Songs:

31   Schmemann A., *For the life of the world: Sacraments and Orthodoxy.* (Crestwood, NY: St. Vladimir's Seminary Press, 1987), 89.

32   St. John Chrysostom, *On Marriage and Family Life*, Roth C.P., trans. (Crestwood, NY: St. Vladimir's Seminary Press, 1986), 263.

Go forth, O daughters of Zion, and see King Solomon with the crown with which his mother crowned him on the day of his wedding, the day of the gladness of his heart (Song 3:11).

When the crowns are placed on the heads of the groom and bride, they appear as a king and a queen, becoming in essence the royalty of their new family.

In heaven, we will see a beautiful scene: "Kings' daughters are among Your honorable women; at Your right hand stands the queen in gold from Ophir" (Ps 45:9).

The crowns are also spiritual gifts that the Church requests for the couple (as we see in the prayers over the crowns).

Finally, the crowns remind us that the husband is the head of his wife, and the wife is the crown of her husband.

"An excellent wife is the crown of her husband, but she who causes shame is like rottenness in his bones" (Pro 12:4).

"For the husband is head of the wife, as also Christ is head of the church; and He is the Savior of the body" (Eph 5:23).

The following prayer from the Byzantine rite alludes to the fact that each has become a crown to the other, and that the bond of marriage is not accomplished merely through rings, but through heavenly crowns. For when the priest places the crowns over the couple's heads, he says: "Your servant (so) is crowned to your servant (so) in the name of the Father, the Son, and the Holy Spirit."

And at the end of the crowning session, the priest concludes, "Accept their crowns in your kingdom."

What does the Coptic Crowning Prayer Include?

The Church prays to God, saying:

"O Holy God, who crowned the saints with unfading crowns... O You our Master, now, also, bless these crowns which we prepared to be set upon Your two servants, to be for them:

"Crowns of glory and honor. Amen.

"Crowns of blessing and salvation. Amen.

"Crowns of Joy and happiness. Amen.

"Crowns of jubilation and delight. Amen.

"Crowns of virtue and justice. Amen.

"Crowns of wisdom and understanding hearts. Amen.

"Crowns of comfort and confirmation. Amen."

Then the priest says a prayer for the well-being of the couple.

Do the Crowns have Spiritual Meaning?

When the crown is placed on the head, it signifies glory and honor. Spiritually, it means that a person is adorned with a special virtue; thus, the virtue becomes a wreath placed on the head. That is why when in praying "crowns of wisdom and understanding hearts," the Church asks God to grant the couple special wisdom and understanding.

Why does the Church Pray for These Virtues in Relation to the Crowns?

The Church asks for hidden permanent virtues to become visible and continuous in the life of the couple, just as a crown is visible. Thus, the Church prays that virtues such as wisdom, justice, understanding, steadfastness, joy, gladness, etc., become visible in the couple's life.

At the same time, the Church asks that God crown them with glory and honor, blessing and salvation, joy and happiness, comfort and grace.

What else would a person need for their family life, once presented with all these virtues, or what more could they ask for? Of course, nothing! Thus, the Church in her love asks for "Whatever things are true, whatever things are noble, whatever things are just, whatever things are pure, whatever things are lovely, whatever things are of good report" (Phil 4:8).

Praying for the Elements of a Successful Life

The Church has asked God to crown the couple not only with all the necessary elements of a spiritual life but also with the elements of a happy married life and a successful life in society. That is why it is important for all the attendees, deacons, and the couple to join in saying "Amen" at the end of each prayer, so that God may graciously hear and bestow these virtues generously. The attendees are an essential part of this prayerful event and should diligently pray that this marriage may continue to prosper, be fruitful, and be a blessing.

The Crowns and Heaven!

The crowns with which the couple are crowned symbolize the crowns they will receive in heaven on the day of "the wedding of the Lamb," as mentioned in Revelation 19:9.

Therefore, rejoice, O you wedded couple. In a heavenly assembly, in the presence of God and of the people, you have received the sign and symbol of the kingdom inheritance, the crowns that await you in eternity, when you endure to the end in peace...

You are on the Lord's path, journeying toward His kingdom... These crowns with which you have been crowned will remain in your minds. They are a vision from afar, an example, and a continual reminder of the blessed eternity that awaits you.

By now, you understand why the Holy Matrimony is called "the Crowning Ceremony."

It is called the Crowning Ceremony because:

✤ The couple wears sanctified crowns.

✤ Praying over the crowns is an essential part of the rite.

✤ Crowning is present in the rites of all Orthodox Churches, both Eastern and Oriental.

✤ The ceremony includes the blessing of the sign of the cross over the robes, crowns, and rings, which is very fundamental in the Crowning Ceremony.

The Blessings While Wearing the Crowns

What beautiful and awesome and reverent moments these are! How bountiful are the blessings of such moments! How deep is the grace bestowed upon the couple!

After the couple wears the crowns, the priest gently brings their heads close together while saying the three blessings:

"Crown them with glory and honor, O Father. Amen. Bless them, O only begotten Son. Amen. Sanctify them, O Holy Spirit. Amen."

In this mystery, the signs of the cross have a significant importance in relation to the mystery. By making the signs of the cross, the name of God is invoked to come, bless, and complete the Mystery: For the Father crowns the couple with glory and honor, the Son blesses them, and the Holy Spirit sanctifies them. And the Holy Spirit descends upon the couple and unites them in one body and one heart.

Now the couple have been robed in sanctified vestments (gowns), anointed with holy oil, crowned with glorious crowns, and the Holy Trinity has completed His mystery in them. When the deacons behold all this, they chant with great jubilation:

"Worthy, worthy, worthy, is the bridegroom and his helpmate."

This proclaims the great heavenly blessings that the couple has been counted worthy of receiving.

Then, the deacons, through the eyes of faith, continue their joyful chanting.

"Unfading crowns, the Lord has granted to this bridegroom, of Jesus Christ."

Then they conclude with this joyful song:

"Be enlightened, be enlightened, O bridegroom and your true bride, in your prepared place. Accept the joy and the gift that our God Christ granted you. Go with joy to your bridal chamber, which is ornamented with varied things."

One Body

Now God has united the bride and bridegroom, making them one body, or just as the Exposition says, "and you became as one person." No one truly knows what the Holy Spirit does to make the two become one!

What is This Grace That Unites the Two Together and Makes the One?

We do not know… this is a mystery. But we witness its result in the words of our Lord Jesus Christ, "Therefore, what God has joined together, let not man separate" (Mt 19:6).

And we believe that the same God who has changed the nature of water into good new wine at the wedding in Cana of Galilee is the One who makes the two into one.

The Holy Spirit has united them forever in an unbreakable unity. How beautiful is this eternal union, whose threads God Himself has woven! How beautiful is this one body, a new creation, a new miracle of creation! Indeed, by every measure, it is a miracle.

In the Mystery of Baptism, a Christian person is born again from the water and the Holy Spirit, born of God, as a new creation. In the Mystery of Holy Matrimony, God takes two baptized persons who are new creations and makes them one in Him in an unfathomable mystery. He himself describes it as: "So then, they are no longer two but one flesh" (Mt 19:6). It is a new miracle of creation, the creation of one out of two. With the descent of the Holy Spirit upon them, they become truly one body.

When we say "one body," it does not merely refer to the physical body; it signifies their complete union together. They "became an integrated human entity," meaning one Christian being.[33] The Lord Jesus Christ summarizes this mystery, saying, "For this reason, a man shall leave his father and mother and be joined to his wife, and the two shall become one flesh" (Mt 19:5).

This is a heavenly invisible gift that the couple feels in the depths of their beings, which is rightly called "the gift of the one body."

---

33   See Dr. Adel Haleem, *The Christian marriage Meaning.* in Arabic (Cairo, Egypt: Youth Bishopric Printing, 1991), 65.

It is a miracle that transforms a man and a woman into a single Christian matrimonial being. The miracle of the marital union between a man and a woman is in the likeness of Christ's union with the Church (Eph 5:25–26).[34]

This is why the mother Church prays multiple times for the unity of the bridegroom and the bride. Here are some examples:

The priest prays in the First Matrimonial Prayer:

"We ask You, also, now, O our King, to join Your servants (…) and (…) to be united to each other in one body, and to enter the law of joy."

The priest prays in the Second Matrimonial Prayer:

"You, also, Good One, the Lover of Mankind, bless the union of Your two servants (…) and (…) who are united to each other according to Your will."

The priest prays in the Third Matrimonial Prayer:

"O Master Lord, look upon Your two servants (…) and (…) his helpmate. Confirm their union."

Again, I say: the depth of this miracle, the strength of this unity, and the permanence of this bond are God's will and the desire of His heart…

---

34   Ibid., 66.

But does a Person Have Freedom of Choice?

Have the bride and groom added the prayers of their hearts to these prayers?

Have they opened their hearts to one another so that the Holy Spirit may lead them to this oneness of heart, goal, and mind? Or do they want to remain two? Each one seeks to prove oneself, to assert one's own existence, and even to impose upon the other what the other does not want or hope for?

God desires this unity, yet sometimes humans resist it. The result can be disagreements and quarrels that begin even on the very first day of marriage.

We sometimes grieve because the newlyweds had the path to joy laid open before them, and God Himself was standing at the door, knocking, ready to offer them the secret of happiness. Yet, by their own will, they refused to open to Him.

May the Lord have mercy. Lord have mercy. Lord have mercy.

Handing over the Bride to the Groom

One of the most beautiful moments is the moment the bride is handed over to the groom. It starts as the deacons chant:

"Receive, O bridegroom, a bride who is yours, Jesus Christ has given her to you, and at the hand of our father the priest, He has presented her to you, and blessed you both with His holy name."

How wonderful is the eye of faith with which the deacons see what is happening: the Lord Christ Himself gives the bride to the bridegroom and He personally blesses them.

At that moment, the priest places the bride's hand into the groom's hand and covers both hands with a white silk veil.

This act of giving the newlyweds to one another by placing one's hand in the hand of the other is an ancient custom rooted in the Holy Bible, as it carries a sign of acceptance and approval before the Church.[35]

In the Old Testament, we see the pious Raguel, when he was about to give his daughter Sarah in marriage to the young Tobias, took her right hand and place it into Tobias's hand, saying, "Behold, receive her according to the decree of Moses" (Tobias 7:13 LXX, The Orthodox Study Bible).

What is the Purpose of the Small White Silk Veil that Covers Their Hands?

Perhaps this small white silk veil that covers the hands of the bride and groom reminds you of the small while silk veil used when partaking of Holy Communion

---

35   See Father Yoohanna Salama, *The Precious Pearls of the Church Rituals*, In Arabic, Part Two, (Cairo, Egypt: St. George Bookstore), 139.

at the end of the Divine Liturgy. Indeed, it is the very same veil used during Communion. It will be used by the bride and groom when they receive Holy Communion, just as was done in the past generations. It is as if the priest is saying to the couple, "The next step for both of you is to partake of Holy Communion together after this service."

In the past, the crowning ceremony was celebrated before the Sunday Divine Liturgy. At its conclusion, the bride and groom were led in a joyful procession through the church. They then remained in the church to attend the Divine Liturgy and receive Holy Communion, using the same white silk veil that the priest had placed over their hands during the ceremony. Thus, while each member of the congregation comes forward to receive Communion holding a small white veil, the bride and groom approach together to receive the Holy Communion, sharing the same white silk veil, a beautiful sign that they have become one.

My brother, the bridegroom, you have not received your bride from a human hand, but from God, for she is God's gift to you. Keep this before your eyes all the days of your life, and listen to what the Church is saying to you in these sacred moments.

Commandment to the Bridegroom

"My blessed son, who is supported by the grace of the Holy Spirit, you are required to receive your wife at this blessed hour with a clear conscience, a pure soul, and a full heart. Excel in doing all that is good for her. Have compassion on her and hasten to do that which gladdens her heart. You have both been crowned with the heavenly crowning and the spiritual marriage. The grace of God has settled upon you. When you accept what has been commanded of you, the Lord will take your hand, increase your livelihood, grant you blessed children by whom God will delight your eyes, grant you a long age and prosperous life, and prosper your outcome in this life and the thereafter."

After this, the deacons chant Psalm 45, which, in the spirit of prophecy, speaks concerning the Church and her Bridegroom, the heavenly King. Through this sacred Psalm, the Church seeks to inscribe upon the bride's heart this important analogy:

✤ The relationship and love of the groom for his bride is like Christ's love for the Church...

✤ The wedding of the bride to her groom resembles a heavenly wedding...

✤ And her obedience as a bride to her groom mirrors the Church's obedience to Christ...

Thus, the deacons chant:

"Hear, O daughter, and see and incline your ear, forget your people, and your father's house because the King has desired your beauty, for He is your Lord."

Then they chant:

"Listen, O bride, understand and incline your ear, for the bridegroom desired your goodness, for he is your husband and is worthy to be listened to."

Sometimes, the deacons do not chant the portion that relates to the Church:

"Hear, O daughter, and see and incline your ear, forget your people, and your father's house, because the King has desired your beauty, for He is your Lord."

However, the original order of the rite required that this portion be chanted first, in order to:

✤ Remind us of the heavenly wedding that awaits us.

✤ Remind us of our Bridegroom, the heavenly King.

✤ Remind the newlyweds that their marriage is established through a mystery like Christ's marriage to the church.

✤ Remind the bride to forget her father's house and become attached to her groom. This is particularly important for the continued peace of the new home.

✤ The church makes the same appeal to the groom when she says: "For this reason, a man shall leave his father and mother and be joined to his wife…" meaning that the groom, too, needs psychological weaning from his parents.

For either the bride or the groom who, after marriage, continues to live under the shadow of their parents and allows them to interfere in their newly married life and household affairs, this can quickly lead to problems. Psychological separation of the newlyweds from their parents is an essential element in establishing a stable new home. Families, therefore, must refrain from interfering in the affairs of the new household and instead pray for the newlyweds, so that these prayers may become a source of peace and stability in their new life together.

Then the Priest Reads the Bride's Commandment

"And you, blessed daughter, and happy bride, you have heard what was commanded of your husband. So you are required to honor and respect him… You must receive him with joy and cheer, do not frown in his face, do not neglect any of his rights upon you, and fear God in all matters with him."

"As you listen to what we commanded you to do, the Lord will take your hand, increase your livelihood, and blessings will descend upon your home, and He will grant you blessed children by whom God will delight your eyes."

Here we see the wisdom of the Church: she does not give a commandment only to the bride, but also to the groom. Notice this beautiful balance in the commandments:

The groom is called to offer tenderness and love, and the bride, in turn, is called to honor him.

The groom must labor diligently for what benefits his bride, and the bride is encouraged to listen to him.

And the groom should hasten to do what delights her heart, and the bride is urged not to withhold any of his due rights.

The Couple Kneeling Before the Altar

The newlyweds leave their place and kneel before the holy altar as the priest offers the closing blessing ...

So, the bridegroom does not receive his bride from the hand of man, but from the hand of God ...

He does not receive his bride in a worldly place, but in the house of God.

And he received her, not in a room attached to the church, but in front of the holy altar ...

The kneeling before the Altar carries many profound meanings:

✛ Before the altar, the couple received one another.

✛ Before the altar, they accept each other as partners for life.

✛ The altar itself stands as a witness to this marriage.

✛ The door of the altar is open before them, symbolizing the opening of the gates of the Kingdom of Heaven to them.

✤ They now behold the beauty and glory of God's altar, a foretaste of the splendor and beauty of the heavenly altar.

✤ Here, as they bow down, kneeling before the altar, in their precious robes and glorious crowns, they express their humble submission to God.

✤ They kneel before the altar to receive the blessings of the holy altar.

✤ Their kneeling before the altar is also a sign of their obedience and their commitment to fulfill all the Church's commandments, which they have heard.

Thus, the altar becomes the last place their eyes see in the church, so that heaven remains what they look forward to for the rest of their life.

Then everyone prays "Our Father who art in Heaven," and the priest prays the three absolutions and concludes with the blessing.

In the current rite, the newlyweds then leave the church in a solemn procession led by the deacons, while they chant in Coptic *Shere Maria Ti-ooro* meaning "Hail to Mary the Queen."

The couple was ushered into the church with the hymn "King of Peace," and they depart with the hymn "Hail to Mary the Queen."

Bibliography

Arabic References

(Arranged from the oldest to the newest)

Ibn Kabar, *The Lantern of Darkness for Clarifying Service*, Second Part, 14th Century, in Arabic, (Cairo, Egypt: Mina Organization for Printing, 1998).

Pope Gabriel the Fifth, *The Order of Rituals*, 15th Century, in Arabic, (Cairo, Egypt: The Franciscan Center for Oriental Studies, 1962).

Father Yoohanna Salama, *The Precious Pearls of the Church Rituals*, Part Two, in Arabic, (Cairo, Egypt: St. George Bookstore).

Hegumen Mankerious Awadallah, *Minaret of Holiness*, the Fifth book, in Arabic, (Cairo, Egypt).

Bishop Gregorius, *The Spiritual Values in the Mystery of Marriage*, in Arabic; (Cairo, Egypt: Bishopric of Higher Theological Studies, Coptic Culture, and Scientific Research).

Hegumen Tadros Yacob Malaty, *Saint Mary in the*

Orthodox Concept, in Arabic, (Alexandria, Egypt: St. George Coptic Orthodox Church, Sporting, 1978).

Dr. Adel Haleem, *The Christian Marriage Meaning*, in Arabic, (Cairo, Egypt: Youth Bishopric Printing, 1991).

English References

Tertullian, *Ante-Nicene Fathers*, 3–4, (Peabody, MA: Hendrickson Publishers, 1994).

Clement of Alexandria. *Fragment on Matthew* 22:12. In *Ante-Nicene Fathers* 8, Roberts A. and Donaldson J., eds. (Buffalo, NY: Christian Literature Publishing Co., 1885).

St. Ambrose, *On the Mysteries. Nicene and Post-Nicene Fathers: Second Series* 10, (Peabody, MA: Hendrickson Publishers,1994).

St. Jerome, *Commentary on Matthew*, Scheck T. P., trans. (Washington, D.C.: Catholic University of America Press, 2008).

St. John Chrysostom, *On Marriage and Family Life*, Roth C. P. & Anderson D., trans. (Crestwood, NY: St. Vladimir's Seminary Press, 1986).

St. John Chrysostom, *Nicene, and Post-Nicene Fathers, First Series* 12–13, (Peabody, MA: Hendrickson Publishers, 1994).

St. John Chrysostom, *Nicene and Post-Nicene*

Fathers: First Series 13, Alexander G., trans; Schaff P., ed. (Buffalo, NY: Christian Literature Publishing Co., 1889).

St. Augustine, *On Marriage, Nicene and Post-Nicene Fathers: First Series* 5, (Peabody, MA: Hendrickson Publishers, 1994).

The Ecumenical Councils, Nicene and Post-Nicene Fathers: Second Series 14, (Peabody, MA: Hendrickson Publishers, 1994).

John Meyendorff, *Marriage, An Orthodox Perspective.* (New York, NY: St. Vladimir's Seminary Press, 1984).

Schmemann A., *For the life of the world: Sacraments and Orthodoxy.* (Crestwood, NY: St. Vladimir's Seminary Press, 1987).

Vikan, Gary. "Early Christian and Byzantine Rings in the Zucker Family Collection." The Journal of the Walters Art Gallery 45, Baltimore, Maryland (1987), 32–43.

H. G. Bishop Moussa, *The Marriage Ceremony,* (Cairo, Egypt: Bishopric of Youth Bookstore).

Bercot D., *A Dictionary of Early Christian Beliefs: A Reference Guide to More Than 700 Topics Discussed by the Early Church Fathers.* (Peabody, MA: Hendrickson Publishers, 1998).